Other books by Eric Hoffman

Poetry
The Transparent Eye (2016)
Forms of Life (2015)
By the Hours (2013)
The American Eye (2011)

Prose
Oppen: A Narrative (2018)

With Nina Goss:
Tearing the World Apart: Bob Dylan and the 21st Century (2017)

With Jason Sacks and Dominick Grace:
Jim Shooter: Conversations (2017)

With Dominick Grace:
Approaching Twin Peaks: Critical Essays on the Original Series (2017)
Seth: Conversations (2015)
Chester Brown: Conversations (2013)
Dave Sim: Conversations (2013)

Eric Hoffman
LOSSES OF LIFE

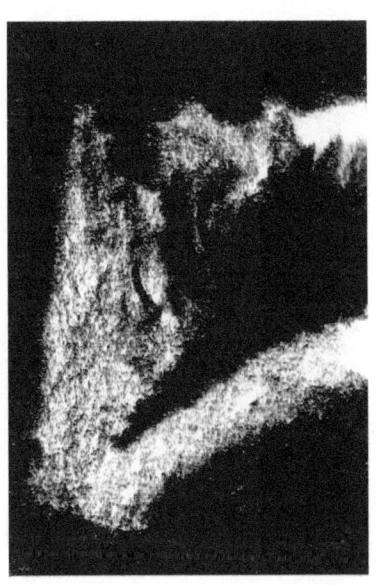

SPUYTEN DUYVIL
New York City

Poems previously published in *Otoliths*. Thanks to Mark Young for including these poems in among the contents of his estimable journal.

©2018 Eric Hoffman

ISBN 978-1-947980-11-2

cover art: t thilleman

Library of Congress Cataloging-in-Publication Data

Names: Hoffman, Eric R., author.
Title: Losses of life / Eric Hoffman.
Description: New York City : Spuyten Duyvil, [2018] | Poems previously
    published in Otoliths in 2017.
Identifiers: LCCN 2017051547 | ISBN 9781947980112 (pbk.)
Classification: LCC PS3608.O47767 A6 2018 | DDC 811/.6--dc23
LC record available at https://lccn.loc.gov/2017051547

CHILD OF MAN 1
STATIONS 33

CHILD OF MAN

from the Journals and Letters
of Ralph Waldo Emerson

Our quaint metaphysical opinions in an hour of anguish like playthings by the bedside of a child deadly sick.
—Samuel Taylor Coleridge, *The Gutch Notebook*

1.

The day my boy was baptized in the old church,
They dressed him in the robe in which they baptized
My brother Charles. A group of departed spirits
Hovered about us, held in Lidian's eyes.

2.

At Plymouth
With its two hundred ponds,
Its hills and slopes
And the great sea-line visible from their peaks —

On the shores of Halfway Pond
We ate our gipsy dinner
And rolled on the beach in the sun,
Dipping our fingers in the cool sand.

We yielded ourselves
To the Italian genius of the time,
The *dolce far niente.*

3.

That night, I went out into the dark
And saw a glimmering star, and heard a frog.
A new scene, a new experience,
The tableau startlingly unique, and temporary.

In spite of all we do, every moment
Forms and disintegrates and in its place
A new occurrence surfaces, its minutiae
An infinite array of specifics and variants.

Each remnant, each shattered piece,
Is precisely replaced, until they reassume
Their fractured fallen positions,
Threadbare hours we manage to salvage
From the calendar's pitiless thresher.

4.

Lidian — whose beauty is her imperfections
(All beauty is imperfection) —
Entered my study and found
The towerlet that Wallie had built
Of two spools, a card, an awl-case,
And a flower-box top,
And fell into such a fit of affection
That she lay down by the structure
And kissed it, declaring
She could possibly stay no longer
But must go off to the nursery
To see with eyes the lovely creature,
And so departed.

5.

Love and awe
A leaf in the forest,
A violet, divine

As the Christ child,
Its blossoming
A transfiguration

Whose perfection
Is its familiarity
And its silence.

6.

Little Waldo cheers the whole house:
Crying out the window

"Pussy-cat, come see Waddow!"
"Little Birdy, come see Waddow!"
"Pies! Fies! Come see me!"

He has brought me a flower
Under the name of "liddel powup."

Lidian shows me two apples
His grandmother gave him.

He held one in each hand
And waited until he was home

Before biting into them,
His teeth leaving a ring of scars

On the apple's skin
As though a small bird
Pecked a perfect oval.

"See where the little angel
Has gnawed them," she said.
"They are worth a barrel of apples
He has not touched."

7.

The boy has two deep blue wells for eyes,
Into which I will gladly peer when I am tired.

Handsome as Walden Pond at sunrise,
He is the darling of the school house

Where he is shouldered and chaired
Every fine day at recess.

8.

A little maiden child is born.
A meek little girl,
And in this short dark winter afternoon
I cannot tell the color of her eyes

Because she keeps them closely shut,
Yet there is nothing in her aspect
That contradicts the hope we seek
That she will be a blessing

For our little company.
Waldo is quite happy
With this fair unexpected apparition
And cannot peep to see her enough.

9.

Waldo watches the dwindling
Of the snow banks
On early grass
For his horse,
That omnipresent Animation
Whereof and whereto
His world is made.

The basket chariot bears away the bell for beauty
But the rackets! and the ninepins!
His hobby-horse has in a fortnight
Grown decrepid and forgotten.

10.

Toys, no doubt, have their philosophy.
Who knows how deep is a boy's delight
In a spinning top?

In playing bat-balls, perhaps
He is charmed with some recognition
Of the movement of planets and stars.

A game of base is of course
An experimental astronomy.
My young master tingles

With a faint sense of being
A tyrannical Jupiter,
Driving spheres madly from their orbit.

11.

We use ten words for every one of the child:
"See the cobwebs go up
Out of the gentleman's mouth."
"The flowers talk when the wind blows over them."

He christens parts of the toy house
With names that have a good sound:
"The interspeglium," "the coridaga" —
Names, he explains, "the children cannot understand."

12.

My little boy grows thin in the hot summer
And runs all to eyes and eyelashes.

"God is glorious," says Waldo.
"He always says his prayers,
And never behaves badly."

When he saw the little dead bird:
"He was gone by-by" and "he was broke."

13.

Heroes do not fix, but flow,
Bend ever forward and invent.
Man is a compendium of nature,

An indomitable savage,
His physique disdains all intrusions,
Lives, wakes, and alters

Amid essences and *billets doux*,
To Himmaleh mountain chains,
Wild cedar swamps

And interior fires,
The molten core of the globe.
Over every chimney is a star

And in the fields an oaken garland
Or a wreath of laurel.
Nature waits to decorate every child.

14.

My boy, my boy is gone.
My angel has vanished,
Fled from my arms like a dream,
And with him all that is glad
And festal and almost social even,
For me, from this world.

All his beauty could not save him.
He gave up his innocent breath
And my world this morning is poor enough.
He adorned the world like a morning star,
And every particular of my life.
I slept in his neighborhood and woke to find him.

I cannot see beyond this fatal occurrence.
I chiefly grieve that I cannot grieve,
That this fact takes no more deep hold
Than other facts, and is dreamlike as they,
A lambent flame that will not burn
Playing on the surface of my river.

15.

The morning of Friday,
I wake at three o'clock
And every cock in the barnyard
Shrills with an unnecessary noise.

And I think of the sinless oxen
Gathered 'round the Christ child
In a simple olive wood manger,
Betraying their quiet indifference —

Those unbounded eyes of sweet indifference —

16.

The sun went up in the morning
With all its yellow and orange light,
Yet the landscape remained
A peculiar blue,
Dishonored by his ongoing absence.

And I found, detestably, I could not resume
The purpose of his bed
And restore to it the swelling of his heart,
Comforted by the presence of Lidian and I,
Waking to find us, massive in the house's small frame,

Crowding its corridors with conversation,
Opening windows and doors
To his prolix imagination,
Amassing a thousand objects
To feed his quiet fascinations,

A parade of passing fancies,
Angels real as stone,
Indians in the shadows,
Titan giants of the sea
Swimming in every teacup.

17.

He had his full swing in the world.
Never, I think, did a child enjoy more —
Playmates, playthings —

Every tramp that ever tramped is abroad
But the little feet are still.
He gave up his innocence
Like a bird.

18.

Must every experience
Only kiss my cheek like the wind
And pass away? I think of Tantalus,

Standing in a pond below the fruit tree,
Branches rising from his grasp,
Waters ebbing when he bends to drink.

It seems I ought to call upon the wind
To describe my boy,
My fast receding boy,

Who decorated for me
The morning star, the evening cloud,
All the particulars of daily economy.

He touched with his lively curiosity
Every trivial fact of circumstance:
The hard coal and soft coal

That I put into my stove;
The wood, of which he carried
His little quota for grandmother's fire;

The hammer, the pincers, and file
He was so eager to use;
The microscope and magnet, the little globe;

Every trinket and instrument,
The loads of gravel in the meadow,
The nests of the hen-house.

For everything he had his own name
And way of thinking.
Every word came mended from his tongue.

19.

The thought pleases me
That he was never degraded,
No soil stained him,
Too precious and unique
To be huddled away into the waste
And prodigality of things.

Yet his image so gentle,
Yet so gentle in hopes,
Blends with every happy moment,
Every fair remembrance.

20.

I delight in the regularity
And the symmetry of his nature.
Calm and wise and wisely happy
The Creative Power looked out from him
And spoke of anything but Chaos
And interruption, signified strength
And gladdening, all uniting life.

What is the moral of the sun
And moon and roses and acorns
Is the moral of that sweet boy's life,
Humanized by blue eyes and infant eloquence.

21.

I am stripped of all generosity.
He was my ornament
And from the greatest patrician
I am become plebeian at a blow.
He gave license to my fancy
Of magnifying each particular,
And what gentleness I found
Was in the little private passages
Between that boy and me,
In giving and taking,
In his coming to draw or play at my study-table,
Or last summer, in his first walks with me
At some distance from the house.

22.

Most of our lives are clothed in silence,
Because it is too fine for speech,
Because it is unexplainable,

Because we do not live as angels
Eager to be introduced
To new perfections.

Time removes us quite surgically,
And what passes for love in this world
Is made official —

Yet sorrow makes us children again,
Destroys all differences of intellect.
The wisest knows nothing.

23.

If I go down to the garden
It seems someone has fallen into the Brook.
Every place is handsome
Or tolerable where he has been.
His house he proposed to build
In the burrs of summer
And winter's snows.
"My music," he said,
"Makes the thunder dance."

"Momma, may I have this bell
Which I have been making
To stand by the side of my bed?
But I am afraid it may sound at night,
Louder than ten thousand hawks.
It will be heard across the water.
It will sound like some great glass thing
Which falls down
And breaks all to pieces."

24.

Ellen asks her grandmother:
"Why can't God stay alone
With the angels a little while
And let Waldo come down to play?"

25.

Life is an inexhaustible treasure of thought,
A pageantry of emotion

That stains us and pulls us down
Into the bitter exchanges of our most foul and stumbling actions,

Our depravities and our shame,
Our guilt and insecurities that pile upon us,

Pitiless as the passing of days
And the hours that crowd our hearts,

Held hostage to our minor triumphs,
Drawing rent from the least of rewards,

And repaying with casks of wine
Those whose cups are already filled.

26.

Creation is proof of the divine,
Sincerity the father of immortality —

To regret without doubt,
Without timidity,

Just as it lies in the consciousness,
The responsibility of facts.

27.

I have seen the poor boy
When he came to a tuft of violets in the wood,
Kneel down, smell them, kiss them,
And depart without plucking.

The chrysalis he brought in
With care and tenderness
And gave to his mother to keep
Is still alive and he,
The most beautiful of all children of men
Is not here.

I comprehend nothing of this fact
But its bitterness.
Explanations none, consolations none
That rise out of the fact itself.
Only diversion, only oblivion of this,
And pursuit of new objects.

28.

Look at that yonder dogwood
Which the sun has drawn out of the ground
By its continual love and striving towards him,
And which now spreads a thousand boughs
In gratitude, basking in his presence.

Does that not see?
It sees all over, with every leaf
And with each new blossom
Unfurls itself into the light
With fresh ecstasy.

Stations

*I'm just a station on your way,
I know I'm not your lover*
    —Leonard Cohen, "Sisters of Mercy"

1.

Sin is a diminution,
A pravity.

The intellect names it shade,
Absence of light, essenceless.

We say what we are,
A telescope focused on objects,

A galvanic circuit chasing extravagance,
Whose magnitude adds nothing.

2.

We grasp at what slips,
The handholds, the footholds—

We reach for others
That also slip and fall away.

3.

To any house
A key can be given
Or rescinded.

We furnish a home
With qualities
We can afford,

Place mirrors
Where reflections are wanted
Or necessity demands.

Some rooms hold horizons
While others invite
Only evening light.

4.

Of what use is fortune or favor
To a cold temperament,
To one whose nature is defective?

They'd die rather than pay their debt,
Or if they live simply
Disappear into the crowd.

5.

Life is a bubble,
Sleep within sleep,
A private dream,

And man a golden impossibility
That threads a little bit of light
From darkness to darkness.

6.

The yellow church lights glow,
The snow-filled streets of Boston
Made blue by moonlight, they too glow—

The carriages cross Main Street,
Past places of business
And the crowds

Move from place to place,
Each alike in appetite,
Yet singular in strength.

The radiance of the church lights
At this frozen hour,
Refuge and surrender.

7.

Tranquil eternal meadows,
Heaven without rent,

And heavenly creatures,
Naked, emblazoned

By desire, bare
Their heavy breasts,

Offer youth
Almost as penitence.

With each new beauty
A thirst is quenched.

Every appetite, once infant pure,
Darkens with lust.

8.

Our love of the real
Draws us to permanence
Yet we anchor in quicksand,

We look at genius once
Then must take leave of it
And never see it again.

The birds alight nowhere,
Hop from bough to bough—
What fortune they have in ignorance.

9.

Amid this vertigo,
I am thankful
For the small mercies.

In the morning I awake
And find again this tired old world,
And even when I climb

Into the thin and cold realm
Of lifeless science, I sink
Into sensation, the equator of life.

10.

Experience is a gradual accretion
Of privation,
An impoverishment of virtue
And wisdom.

At times time's contents
Seem routine and genius
A chance occurrence.

The ships at a distance
Are romantic,
Yet on board we hear the groans
Of a sea-beaten wood,

We see the mussel-crowded hulls
And salt-bruised sails,
We smell the rich mold that perfumes
These heroic journeys.

11.

The hill is held together by its roots,
The pleasant sun-painted hills,

And the houses upon them seem at peace
Until their roofs are lifted.

12.

We cultivate pain—
An omnipresent state—
A toxic fermentation.

Hoping to know the world better
By its bitter taste,
We find grief curiously empty.

The mind never touches its object
And the heart remains unconstrained
On an unnavigable sea.

Those who lose a beautiful estate,
A home, a wife, or child,
Cannot bring their grief any nearer.

It falls away, and eventually leaves
Little scar or trace.
The wisest welcome this disaster.

They know the hottest conflagrations
Cool into ash.
They are blessed

With an unrelenting acceptance
That life is a poverty of knowledge.
We learn too late.

The one consolation
Is to live in defiance of this.
The rest is decoration.

13.

The untiring conquerors
For all their rapaciousness

Retire silently to ungracious graves
And weep to be forgotten.

Their ruins are the unmet victories
Of the proud. We worship them

As monuments
When the weak hearts

Of shopkeepers
Are as noble as any crown.

14.

Truth is an agreement,
Two opposing globes
Touching at a single minor point.

Appetency increases
The longer they remain in orbit,
Their equal energies opposed.

The eye makes the horizon.

15.

God walks among the vagabonds
Who know his son died

Suffering the banalities of wounds
Less torturous

Than a father's abandonment
When desperate for his love,

That he hurled himself headlong
Into a self-made hell

To suffer the torments
Of his own creation.

What is the mystery
When we are abandoned only

When doubt is undoubtable
And love is preliminary to pain?

16.

The gardens are dressed
At midnight. The gentle
Fog lifts in the morning,

Revealing its fruits,
A dark loam gifted
With rich sustenance.

The household is met
At the morning table.
We see each other age

Before our eyes.
We watch the children grow.
All this is forgotten

Save for vague memories
Or when lost regained
In terrible detail, until

It finally ripens
Into a bitter fruit,
Becomes the meal

That fills the table,
An absent blessing,
Present as a wound.

Eric Hoffman is the author of several collections of poetry, including *The Transparent Eye* (Spuyten Duyvil, 2016), and *Forms of Life* (2015), *By the Hours* (2013), and *The American Eye* (2011), published by Dos Madres Press. He is the author of *Oppen: A Narrative*, a biography of poet George Oppen (Spuyten Duyvil, 2018), editor of *Cerebus the Barbarian Messiah: Essays on the Epic Graphic Satire of Dave Sim and Gerhard* (McFarland, 2012), co-editor (with Dominick Grace) of *Approaching Twin Peaks: Essays on the Original Series* (McFarland, 2017), *Dave Sim: Conversations* (2013), *Chester Brown: Conversations* (2013), and *Seth: Conversations* (2015), with Grace and Jason Sacks of *Jim Shooter: Conversations* (2017), and with Nina Goss of *Tearing the World Apart: Bob Dylan and the 21st Century* (2017), all published by the University Press of Mississippi. He lives in Connecticut with his wife Robin and son Sailor.

www.ingramcontent.com/pod-product-compliance
Lightning Source LLC
Chambersburg PA
CBHW021159080526
44588CB00008B/413